DIPLOMATIC INSULTS FOR EVERYDAY USE

A Handbook of Polite Offense and Elegant Sarcasm

ISBN 9798269862996
@ 2025 Casper Frankie Shard

Why I Wrote This Book

I wrote Diplomatic Insults after realizing that my greatest achievements in self-control were often mistaken for silence.

This book was born in that sacred space between wanting to scream and deciding to sound superior instead.

It's for those of us who have mastered the art of the raised eyebrow, the meaningful pause, and the perfectly-timed "Interesting."
You've earned a manual — not for anger management, but for elegant survival.

This isn't therapy.
It's emotional fencing.
And you, dear reader, are about to become Olympic-level.

Introduction

If you've ever bitten your tongue so hard it deserved hazard pay — congratulations, you've come to the right place.

Each Session in this book is your personal appointment with serenity and sass. You'll find:

* Session Goal: A reminder that we're pretending this is self-improvement.
* Diagnosis: A polite label for your current emotional meltdown.
* Therapist's Note: Because sarcasm heals faster when it's formatted nicely.
* Recommended Responses: A curated list of things to say when you could destroy someone but choose wisdom instead.
* Progress Check: A tiny pat on the back for surviving society one polite sigh at a time.

You can read these Sessions in order, skip around, or use them as guided meditations when you're trapped in conversations that make you question civilization.

And that extra white space?
That's intentional. It's for you — to jot down your own graceful retorts, design future comebacks, or doodle your therapist's shocked face.

Now take a deep breath. Straighten your posture. You're about to practice the rare art of staying classy while being this close to chaos.

Your therapy begins now.

Session 1: Maintaining Composure While Questioning Humanity

Session Goal:
To remain calm and professional when confronted with extraordinary levels of confusion.

Diagnosis:
A recurring belief that common sense is optional.

Therapist's Note:
Remember, we don't fix people. We observe them — like rare wildlife — from a safe emotional distance.

Recommended Responses:

- "That's an... original interpretation of reality."

- "Fascinating logic. I'll need a moment to process it."

- "You make confidence look effortless."

- "I admire your commitment to that point of view."

Progress Check:
If you managed to say any of the above without sighing audibly, that's real growth.

Session 2: Finding Peace in the Sound of Repeated Mistakes

Session Goal:
To stay serene while watching history repeat itself — loudly.

Diagnosis:
Chronic déjà vu caused by others' refusal to learn.

Therapist's Note:
Patience isn't about waiting calmly. It's about waiting stylishly.

Recommended Responses:

- "We've been here before — must be our favorite spot."

- "Practice makes... almost perfect."

- "Oh, we're doing this again? Excellent. I needed the reminder."

- "Consistency really is your strong suit."

Progress Check:
You may now reward yourself with coffee, silence, or both.

Session 3: Responding Gracefully to the Utterly Illogical

Session Goal:
To respond intelligently to statements that make no sense — without breaking eye contact.

Diagnosis:
Temporary logic paralysis.

Therapist's Note:
Not every argument deserves a counterargument. Some deserve applause — for creativity.

Recommended Responses:

- "I see where you're coming from. It's... a place."

- "You've truly redefined the concept of 'interesting.'"

- "That's a brave conclusion."

- "Let's agree to admire your confidence."

Progress Check:
When you stop correcting people mid-sentence and start documenting quotes for future entertainment, you've reached enlightenment.

Session 4: Meetings – The Art of Looking Engaged While Dissociating

---

Session Goal:
To survive long meetings without biting anything, including your tongue.

Diagnosis:
Information overload, empathy underflow.

Therapist's Note:
Active listening doesn't always require actual listening.

Recommended Responses:

- "Excellent point. Let's circle back... someday."

- "Could you repeat that? I was mesmerized by your confidence."

- "Let's add that to the growing list of things we'll never do."

- "Such clarity. Almost poetic."

Progress Check:

You're cured when you can smile through a PowerPoint without spontaneous eye-rolling.

Session 5: Family Gatherings and Other Endurance Tests

Session Goal:

To remain gracious while fielding life advice from people who think Wi-Fi is a medical condition.

Diagnosis:

Inherited patterns of polite suffering.

Therapist's Note:

Remember, the secret to family diplomacy is simple: never argue with someone who proudly begins every sentence with "In my day."

Recommended Responses:

- "You always know how to make things... interesting."

- "That's certainly one way to see it."

- "I appreciate your input. I'll treasure it privately."

- "Oh, you still remember that story. How... persistent."

Progress Check:
If you can leave the table without explaining your life choices, congratulations — your therapy is working.

Session 6: Compliments That Aren't, and How to Receive Them Anyway

Session Goal:
To accept questionable compliments with grace and minimal eyebrow movement.

Diagnosis:
Compliment Confusion Syndrome (CCS): the inability to tell if "You look so awake today!" is praise or warning.

Therapist's Note:
Sometimes people mean well. Other times, they mean words.

Recommended Responses:

- "Thank you! I do try to look vaguely functional."

- "How sweet — I'll choose to take that positively."

- "Oh, that's... specific."

- "You say the nicest things when you're not thinking."

Progress Check:
When you can smile and move on without replaying the moment three hours later, you've achieved emotional maturity.

Session 7: Emails That Begin with 'Per My Last Message'

Session Goal:
To express assertiveness while sounding as though you still believe in teamwork.

Diagnosis:
Chronic Inbox Tension with passive-aggressive tendencies.

Therapist's Note:
Every "Per my last message" is just "Can you read?" in a nicer font.

Recommended Responses:

- "Just bringing this back to your attention — again."

- "Following up in case my last message mysteriously evaporated."

- "Gentle reminder, delivered with the strength of ten sighs."

- "Appreciate your time. Especially the time it took not to reply."

Progress Check:

You've mastered communication when you can hit 'Send' calmly, knowing your tone says everything your words don't.

Session 8: How to Smile While Screaming Internally

Session Goal:
To maintain an approachable expression when your soul is quietly leaving the building.

Diagnosis:
Chronic Politeness Fatigue (CPF): caused by excessive smiling during nonsense.

Therapist's Note:
Smiling isn't about happiness — it's about teeth management.

Recommended Responses:

- "I love that for you."

- "What an... unexpected choice."

- "Wow, that's... a sentence."

- "You make optimism look brave."

Progress Check:
If your smile lasts longer than your patience, you've achieved professional serenity.

Session 9: Professional Politeness and Other Forms of Survival

Session Goal:
To stay civil while your brain politely leaves the chat.

Diagnosis:
Overexposure to corporate positivity. Side effects include forced enthusiasm and selective hearing.

Therapist's Note:
Politeness is the art of saying nothing beautifully.

Recommended Responses:

- "That's a fascinating initiative. Let's see where it goes."

- "Absolutely. I love that you're thinking… differently."

- "We'll keep that idea in the parking lot. Forever."

- "I'm so inspired. Truly. Deeply. Theatrically."

Progress Check:
You're stable when you can say "That's great!" without rolling your eyes audibly.

Session 10: Customer Service Zen — Finding Calm Among the Clueless

Session Goal:
To remain kind while humanity tests your Wi-Fi, patience, and faith in evolution.

Diagnosis:
Repeated exposure to the phrase, "Can I speak to your manager?"

Therapist's Note:
Remember: customers are always right — in their own little universes.

Recommended Responses:

- "I completely understand. I just don't agree."

- "That's an excellent question. Not relevant, but excellent."

- "I'd love to help you, once I recover from that sentence."

- "Let's take a deep breath together. You first."

Progress Check:
If you can end the call with "Have a wonderful day" and mean less than 10% of it — you're healed.

Session 11: When "Bless Your Heart" Isn't Quite Enough

Session Goal:
To maintain dignity when your patience runs on fumes.

Diagnosis:
Acute Civility Strain (ACS): caused by excessive exposure to cheerful nonsense.

Therapist's Note:
Kindness is powerful. So is quiet restraint. Use both sparingly.

Recommended Responses:

- "You're absolutely right — in your world."

- "That's so... you."

- "I admire your confidence in saying that publicly."

- "A fascinating conclusion. Truly unexpected."

Progress Check:

If you can say "Bless your heart" and mean none of it, you've reached emotional fluency.

Session 12: Family Diplomacy — Love, Advice, and Selective Hearing

Session Goal:
To navigate conversations that begin with, "You know what you should do…"

Diagnosis:
Familial Overfamiliarity Disorder. Symptoms include unsolicited advice and casserole.

Therapist's Note:
Listening is an art. Pretending to listen is a performance.

Recommended Responses:

- "That's such an interesting approach — for someone else."

- "I appreciate your concern. I'll definitely not act on it."

- "You're right. I should do everything differently."

- "Your consistency is truly admirable."

Progress Check:

If you can smile through the tenth repetition of "Back in my day..." without a single twitch, you're ready for the holidays.

Session 13: Small Talk — The Longest Five Minutes of Your Life

---

Session Goal:
To survive conversations about weather, traffic, and "how busy everyone is."

Diagnosis:
Chronic Conversational Fatigue. Often triggered by phrases like "Crazy day, huh?"

Therapist's Note:
Remember: small talk isn't about meaning — it's about noise management.

Recommended Responses:

- "Oh, absolutely. The weather has been... weathering."

- "Yes, time really does keep moving."

- "Busy? Constantly. Productive? Emotionally."

- "I love these deep conversations. So healing."

Progress Check:

You may leave once you've smiled for the appropriate number of seconds. (Hint: 20.)

Session 14: Parties — Where Introverts Practice Advanced Breathing Techniques

---

Session Goal:
To appear sociable while mentally planning your escape.

Diagnosis:
Social Overstimulation with traces of regret.

Therapist's Note:
Fake it till you make it — or until someone blocks the exit.

Recommended Responses:

- "Such a great turnout. I almost didn't come."

- "I'm having fun. You can tell by my stillness."

- "So many people I can't wait to forget by morning."

- "This playlist really captures the chaos of the human spirit."

Progress Check:
If you've smiled, nodded, and escaped within an hour — you've mastered social balance.

Session 15: When You've Outgrown the Drama (But Still Observe It Casually)

Session Goal:
To let people be wrong in peace.

Diagnosis:
Emotional Overachievement. You've evolved, they haven't.

Therapist's Note:
Wisdom is realizing not every hill is worth the high heels.

Recommended Responses:

- "That's one way to interpret reality."

- "You seem very confident in that conclusion."

- "Growth looks different on everyone."

- "I love that journey for you — from afar."

Progress Check:
When you can scroll past nonsense without screenshotting it for friends, you're nearly healed.

Session 16: The Art of Calmly Not Caring

Session Goal:
To achieve emotional neutrality while appearing deeply invested.

Diagnosis:
Post-Passion Clarity. A beautiful side effect of simply not giving a damn.

Therapist's Note:
Peace isn't found. It's scheduled. Preferably after naps.

Recommended Responses:

- "I'll reflect on that. Briefly."

- "Oh, I stopped worrying about that — it was liberating."

- "That used to bother me. Then I hydrated."

- "Your urgency is impressive. I'm staying calm for balance."

Progress Check:
If your pulse doesn't rise when chaos enters the room, congratulations — you've ascended.

Session 17: Polite Revenge — When Karma's Taking Too Long

Session Goal:
To maintain class while silently wishing the universe efficiency.

Diagnosis:
Delayed Justice Fatigue.

Therapist's Note:
You don't need revenge when irony does home delivery.

Recommended Responses:

- "No worries, time's got this."

- "I'm sure they'll figure it out eventually."

- "Oh, how interesting — consequences take their time."

- "The universe always remembers. I don't need to."

Progress Check:
You've reached peak serenity when you can smile knowing poetic justice is just on backorder.

Session 18: The Self-Aware Ego

Session Goal:
To embrace confidence without needing applause (well, not loudly).

Diagnosis:
Healthy Arrogance: balanced, moisturized, unbothered.

Therapist's Note:
It's not arrogance if it's accurate.

Recommended Responses:

- "Yes, I am aware of my excellence. Thank you for noticing."

- "Confidence isn't noise — it's posture."

- "I'm not competing. I'm existing fabulously."

- "Validation? Oh, I'm outsourcing that now."

Progress Check:
When your worth isn't up for debate, you're untouchable.

Session 19: Tranquil Pessimism — Expecting Less, Enjoying More

Session Goal:
To find serenity through adjusted expectations.

Diagnosis:
Chronic Realism. Untreatable but oddly comforting.

Therapist's Note:
Optimism is nice. Realism comes with snacks.

Recommended Responses:

- "I'm not negative. I'm just pre-disappointed."

- "Hope for the best, but dress for chaos."

- "It's not cynicism, it's experience."

- "Miracles happen. Just... not often."

Progress Check:
You're cured when you can laugh at disaster and mean it.

Session 20: Zen Level — Fluent in Calm Sarcasm

Session Goal:
To exist in peace, sip your coffee, and observe madness as art.

Diagnosis:
Enlightened Detachment: the final form.

Therapist's Note:
You can't control the world. But you can narrate it beautifully.

Recommended Responses:

- "Ah, the universe is improvising again."

- "Everything's fine — or at least aesthetic."

- "I choose peace. And subtle judgment."

- "Namaste — in my lane."

Progress Check:
When your silence speaks louder than your sarcasm, therapy is complete.

Session 21: The Meeting That Could've Been a Memo

Session Goal:

To preserve your will to live during yet another hour of scheduled nothing.

Diagnosis:

Attention Deficit from Excessive Corporate Air.

Therapist's Note:

If it's your fifth "quick sync" of the day, it's not communication — it's captivity.

Recommended Responses:

- "Great discussion. I'll pretend to take notes."

- "We've really explored that... thoroughly."

- "Let's circle back to this when it becomes relevant."

- "Fascinating. Still irrelevant, but fascinating."

Progress Check:

If you can mute yourself, smile, and mentally redecorate your apartment — you've mastered survival.

Session 22: Team-Building Without Emotional Injury

Session Goal:

To feign enthusiasm while strangers shout "trust falls!" near your personal space.

Diagnosis:

Forced Fun Fatigue (FFF). Common in offices with "positive energy."

Therapist's Note:

Remember: the only thing you should fall for at work is paid time off.

Recommended Responses:

- "Wow, I've never bonded this uncomfortably before."

- "So glad we're pretending to enjoy this."

- "Trust me — I'll pass."

- "What a great exercise in tolerance."

Progress Check:
If you survived the icebreaker without eye contact or injury, that's growth.

Session 23: Email Etiquette for the Emotionally Drained

Session Goal:
To write professional messages that hide existential despair.

Diagnosis:
Chronic CC Anxiety with passive-aggressive tendencies.

Therapist's Note:
Every "Just checking in!" is a cry for closure.

Recommended Responses:

- "As per my last message (and emotional limit)."

- "Following up before I lose hope entirely."

- "Gentle reminder that this is still unresolved — like my patience."

- "Looping everyone in, because chaos loves company."

Progress Check:
You're emotionally stable if you can read "Kind regards" and not flinch.

Session 24: When Your Boss Discovers the Word 'Synergy'

Session Goal:
To appear inspired while listening to corporate poetry.

Diagnosis:
Vision Statement Vertigo.

Therapist's Note:
"Synergy" means "We don't know what we're doing, but we'll do it together."

Recommended Responses:

- "Love the enthusiasm — so conceptual."

- "That's a bold use of the word 'strategy.'"

- "I see we're reinventing the obvious again."

- "Such a visionary... collection of syllables."

Progress Check:
If you can nod meaningfully without making a sound, you've mastered executive silence.

Session 25: Feedback That Feels Like a Threat

Session Goal:
To receive "constructive criticism" without constructing a defense.

Diagnosis:
Compliment Anxiety with undertones of restrained violence.

Therapist's Note:
Feedback is just opinion with PowerPoint formatting.

Recommended Responses:

- "Thank you — I'll definitely reflect on that... eventually."

- "Great insight. I hadn't considered being entirely different."

- "Always nice to hear what I could've done last week."

- "I value your perspective. Deeply. Quietly. Resentfully."

Progress Check:
You're healing if you can say "That's helpful" without biting your tongue.

Session 26: The Art of Not Texting First

Session Goal:
To resist the urge to initiate communication with those who enjoy emotional hide-and-seek.

Diagnosis:
Attachment Ambiguity, triggered by typing bubbles.

Therapist's Note:
Remember: silence is also a text. A louder one.

Recommended Responses:

- *No response. It's performance art.*

- "Oh, I thought we were practicing distance."

- "How lovely to hear from you after your sabbatical in ignorance."

- "I was just about to forget you existed."

Progress Check:
You're thriving when unread messages no longer itch.

Session 27: Managing Expectations — Yours, Mostly

Session Goal:
To protect your peace by lowering the bar elegantly.

Diagnosis:
Chronic Optimism Relapse.

Therapist's Note:
Expect less. That way, you'll never be disappointed — only pleasantly underwhelmed.

Recommended Responses:

- "I no longer expect miracles, just mild cooperation."

- "Hope is cute, but I prefer realism."

- "My expectations are on vacation."

- "If it goes well, I'll act surprised."

Progress Check:
If "whatever happens, happens" sounds soothing — you're healing.

Session 28: How to Pretend You Didn't Care Anyway

Session Goal:

To appear emotionally unbothered while your playlist says otherwise.

Diagnosis:

Post-Disappointment Performance Disorder.

Therapist's Note:

Detachment is just caring slowly.

Recommended Responses:

- "Oh, that? Barely noticed."

- "I'm fine. Emotionally minimalist, even."

- "It's giving... indifference."

- "My therapist would be proud of my detachment."

Progress Check:
If your tone stays flat while your playlist cries, you've achieved serenity.

Session 29: Emotional Boundaries, but Make Them Decorative

Session Goal:

To maintain distance while looking approachable.

Diagnosis:

Overextended Empathy with aesthetic tendencies.

Therapist's Note:

A boundary can be firm *and* cute.

Recommended Responses:

- "That sounds hard — for you."

- "I'd love to help, but I've retired from fixing people."

- "My peace doesn't include guest access."

- "Oh, I'm fully booked for emotional labor this quarter."

Progress Check:
If you can say "no" and still sleep well, you're enlightened.

Session 30: When You Want Closure But Settle for Coffee

Session Goal:
To accept caffeine as the universe's apology.

Diagnosis:
Unresolved Feelings with traces of self-awareness.

Therapist's Note:
Sometimes closure looks like espresso and composure.

Recommended Responses:

- "No, no closure needed — caffeine works fine."

- "I'll process this... with whipped cream."

- "Ah, healing through bitter liquids again."

- "Each sip brings me closer to acceptance."

Progress Check:
If you can sip, smile, and not text them later — you've grown.

Session 31: How to Avoid People Without Making It Obvious

Session Goal:
To vanish socially while maintaining plausible deniability.

Diagnosis:
Introvert Burnout with stealth tendencies.

Therapist's Note:
You're not avoiding — you're preserving.

Recommended Responses:

- "Oh, I must've missed that invite — spiritually."

- "We definitely should catch up... next century."

- "I was there in spirit, and my spirit was tired."

- "Let's keep this friendship minimal and meaningful."

Progress Check:
When people stop expecting you and still like you — that's mastery.

Session 32: When Someone Says "We Should Catch Up"

Session Goal:
To agree politely while committing to absolutely nothing.

Diagnosis:
Casual Obligation Fatigue.

Therapist's Note:
"Let's catch up" is just social foreplay for ..never.

Recommended Responses:

- "Yes, absolutely! Sometime after the next apocalypse."

- "That sounds wonderful — I'll check my lifetime availability."

- "Let's pencil that in for 'eventually.'"

- "Oh, the intention was enough. No need to actually meet."

Progress Check:
If you can agree to future plans without opening

Session 33: Compliment Inflation and How to Survive It

Session Goal:
To receive exaggerated praise without developing performance anxiety.

Diagnosis:
Sincerity Deficiency Disorder (SDD).

Therapist's Note:
Not every "You're amazing!" requires belief — sometimes it's just noise with good intentions.

Recommended Responses:

- "You're too kind — and possibly too generous."

- "Oh, please. Tell me more slowly."

- "Wow, that's… a strong opinion."

- "I'm flattered. Confused, but flattered."

Progress Check:
If you can smile and not fact-check the compliment, you're healing.

Session 34: Handling "Just Being Honest" People

Session Goal:
To respond calmly when honesty feels like a weapon.

Diagnosis:
Unsolicited Opinion Exposure.

Therapist's Note:
Honesty without empathy is just rudeness in business casual.

Recommended Responses:

- "Thank you for your bravery in saying that out loud."

- "What a bold way to contribute nothing."

- "Honesty is your hobby, I see."

- "Ah, feedback from the uninvited sector."

Progress Check:
You've mastered composure when your tone says "Noted" and your eyes say "Perish."

Session 35: Public Smiling for Beginners

Session Goal:
To smile convincingly while your soul rehearses its exit strategy.

Diagnosis:
Grin Fatigue, often chronic in service industries.

Therapist's Note:
A smile is the universal way to say "Please stop talking."

Recommended Responses:

- *Smile.* (If necessary, add a nod for emphasis.)

- "Mmm, yes. Incredible."

- "I love that for you."

- "You're so right. In your own way."

Progress Check:
If you can smile through nonsense without face cramps, you've ascended.

Session 36: Laundry Philosophy — Accepting the Infinite Cycle

Session Goal:
To find meaning between rinse and repeat.

Diagnosis:
Domestic Existentialism.

Therapist's Note:
Laundry is life: you'll never be done, and that's the point.

Recommended Responses:

- "It's amazing how my clothes multiply while I sleep."

- "Folding is my cardio, my meditation, my despair."

- "Each sock is a metaphor for loss."

- "If I ignore it, maybe it'll evolve into a new species."

Progress Check:
You've reached enlightenment when the pile no longer haunts you — just decorates your chair.

Session 37: Dishes, Deadlines, and Existential Despair

Session Goal:
To wash plates without crying about capitalism.

Diagnosis:
Mundane Task Melancholia.

Therapist's Note:
You can't scrub away the feeling of futility, but at least your dishes will sparkle.

Recommended Responses:

- "Soap, rinse, question existence, repeat."

- "The dishes aren't the problem. Life is."

- "This sponge has seen things."

- "At least I'm achieving something today."

Progress Check:
If you can hum while cleaning, that's progress — or denial.

Session 38: How to Clean Without Resentment (A Myth)

Session Goal:
To maintain serenity while doing chores no one notices.

Diagnosis:
Domestic Delusion Syndrome.

Therapist's Note:
Cleanliness is next to godliness, but bitterness is closer.

Recommended Responses:

- "I clean, therefore I seethe."

- "Yes, it's spotless — just like my will to live."

- "I love cleaning. Said no one, sincerely."

- "Look how organized I am — emotionally, not so much."

Progress Check:
If you can mop without muttering, you've reached sainthood.

Session 39: When the Wi-Fi Fails but You Keep Breathing

Session Goal:
To survive technological collapse with grace.

Diagnosis:
Connectivity Panic Disorder.

Therapist's Note:
When Wi-Fi fails, your true personality appears.

Recommended Responses:

- "Maybe the universe wants me offline. Rude."

- "Ah, a moment for reflection — and rage."

- "I guess I'll... read?"

- "If I reboot the router and my faith, maybe one will work."

Progress Check:
You're spiritually advanced when you can unplug willingly.

Session 40: Grocery Shopping as a Spiritual Exercise

Session Goal:
To navigate chaos with a calm face and a full cart.

Diagnosis:
Aisle Anxiety, Stage 3: Frozen Foods.

Therapist's Note:
Inner peace is aisle seven — if it's not out of stock.

Recommended Responses:

- "Yes, I'll just stand here and reevaluate life by the bananas."

- "Shopping carts are just bumpers for emotional collisions."

- "The checkout line is a metaphor for patience."

- "I'm buying snacks. For coping, not sharing."

Progress Check:
If you didn't abandon your cart halfway, you've evolved.

Session 41: The Art of Ignoring Group Chats Gracefully

Session Goal:

To achieve digital invisibility without starting drama.

Diagnosis:

Message Overload with passive guilt.

Therapist's Note:

Muting is self-care, not betrayal.

Recommended Responses:

- *Seen.*

- "Just catching up on 483 messages — love that for us."

- "Haha! (in case I missed context)"

- "You all said it perfectly, so I didn't need to."

Progress Check:
You're free when you mute the chat and feel no remorse.

Session 42: Social Media Serenity — Scrolling Without Screaming

Session Goal:
To scroll calmly through curated chaos.

Diagnosis:
Comparison Syndrome with self-esteem lag.

Therapist's Note:
Everyone's life online looks better because it's fictional.

Recommended Responses:

- "Ah, another engagement. How inspiring."

- "Look at that vacation. My plants died."

- "Such productivity. I blinked twice today."

- "Scrolling mindfully — like emotional cardio."

Progress Check:
You're balanced when you can double-tap and mean nothing.

Session 43: Phone Calls — A Prehistoric Anxiety Revival

Session Goal:
To survive the horror of an unexpected ringtone.

Diagnosis:
Unprepared Communication Disorder.

Therapist's Note:
A call is just a text that escaped containment.

Recommended Responses:

- "Oh no, it's talking live."

- "Who still uses voices?"

- "Can this be an email wrapped in silence?"

- "You called? I was emotionally unavailable."

Progress Check:
You've evolved when you answer calmly — or not at all.

Session 44: Notifications That Spark Existential Dread

Session Goal:
To accept that every ding brings either joy or doom.

Diagnosis:
Alert-Induced Anxiety (AIA).

Therapist's Note:
Peace ends the moment your phone buzzes.

Recommended Responses:

- "Oh, a message — from destiny or debt?"

- "If it's important, it'll call twice. Probably."

- "I'll read it when my heart rate drops."

- "Airplane mode: the adult pacifier."

Progress Check:
You're stable when you can ignore the sound and still breathe evenly.

Session 45: Finding Peace in Low Expectations

Session Goal:
To embrace tranquility through the power of not expecting much.

Diagnosis:
Chronic Disappointment Recovery.

Therapist's Note:
Peace begins when standards end.

Recommended Responses:

- "It's fine, I didn't expect it to make sense anyway."

- "Surprise me, but keep it mild."

- "I'm managing expectations like a professional pessimist."

- "My bar is underground, and it's comfortable there."

Progress Check:
If "whatever" sounds meditative now, you're cured.

Session 46: The Zen of Not Caring (Selectively)

Session Goal:
To stop attending every argument you're invited to.

Diagnosis:
Emotional Overinvolvement Syndrome.

Therapist's Note:
You can't control everything — but you can choose your chaos.

Recommended Responses:

- "I see your point, I just don't wish to visit it."

- "You're right — for your universe."

- "I'm conserving my energy for snacks."

- "My peace is louder than your drama."

Progress Check:
If you can walk away mid-debate and smile, enlightenment is achieved.

Session 47: Embracing Chaos Without Setting Fire to It

Session Goal:
To coexist with nonsense without contributing to it.

Diagnosis:
Overreaction Fatigue.

Therapist's Note:
Sometimes the only calm in the storm is your sarcasm.

Recommended Responses:

- "Ah yes, another day, another circus."

- "I'm observing, not participating."

- "This is fine. Emotionally smoky, but fine."

- "My therapist calls this 'growth.' I call it 'suppression.'"

Progress Check:
You're growing when your chaos tolerance beats your caffeine intake.

Session 48: The Universe Doesn't Hate You — It's Just Disorganized

Session Goal:

To stop taking cosmic inconvenience personally.

Diagnosis:

Existential Ego Syndrome.

Therapist's Note:

It's not fate. It's scheduling errors at the universal level.

Recommended Responses:

- "Ah, destiny's on break again."

- "The stars aren't against me — they're just distracted."

- "Retrograde isn't my problem; it's my excuse."

- "Maybe the universe needs therapy too."

Progress Check:
You've evolved when you laugh at the chaos and move on (slowly).

Session 49: Mindfulness for People Who Overthink It

Session Goal:
To be present without overanalyzing the concept of presence.

Diagnosis:
Awareness Overload.

Therapist's Note:
You can't "mindfully" fix what coffee has already solved.

Recommended Responses:

- "I'm here, I think. Wait, am I doing it right?"

- "Breathing. Questioning. Breathing again."

- "I'm present — but mentally in pajamas."

- "Namaste, but sarcastically."

Progress Check:
You're balanced when your inner monologue stops needing subtitles.

Session 50: Weathering Your Mood Like a Forecast

Session Goal:
To let emotional rain happen without moving to another country.

Diagnosis:
Seasonal Sarcasm Disorder.

Therapist's Note:
Some days are cloudy. That's not failure — it's atmosphere.

Recommended Responses:

- "Partly functional with a chance of tears."

- "I'm emotionally overcast, not broken."

- "It's fine, I'm just processing humidity."

- "Today's forecast: mild irritation and dramatic sighs."

Progress Check:
You've healed when you can name your mood without apologizing for it.

Session 51: Emotional Minimalism — Owning Less Drama

Session Goal:
To declutter your feelings like an overstuffed closet.

Diagnosis:
Sentimental Hoarding.

Therapist's Note:
You don't have to feel *everything* to be real.

Recommended Responses:

- "This emotion doesn't spark joy — deleting."

- "I'm keeping calm and donating chaos."

- "My baggage is now in my carry-on."

- "Peace takes less space."

Progress Check:
If your emotional home feels roomier, congratulations — you're zen.

Session 52: Self-Reflection Without Self-Roasting

Session Goal:
To look inward without turning it into stand-up comedy.

Diagnosis:
Introspective Sarcasmosis.

Therapist's Note:
Not every flaw needs a punchline.

Recommended Responses:

- "Yes, I'm self-aware — tragically so."

- "Working on myself, but the update keeps failing."

- "Progress is slow, but so am I."

- "I'm emotionally buffering. Please wait."

Progress Check:
When you can reflect without wincing, that's growth.

Session 53: The Art of Doing Nothing — Proudly

Session Goal:
To find fulfillment in inactivity.

Diagnosis:
Productivity Guilt.

Therapist's Note:
Doing nothing is doing something — it's called existing.

Recommended Responses:

- "I'm resting aggressively."

- "Currently mastering the art of horizontal meditation."

- "I could, but I won't."

- "Stillness is my rebellion."

Progress Check:
You're spiritually advanced when you nap without guilt.

Session 54: How to Believe in Yourself (Ironically)

Session Goal:
To fake confidence until it's convincing.

Diagnosis:
Imposter Realism.

Therapist's Note:
You're not underqualified — just dramatically modest.

Recommended Responses:

- "I believe in myself, selectively."

- "Confidence: 60% performance, 40% caffeine."

- "If I don't know what I'm doing, neither does anyone else."

- "Delusional? No, just optimistic with style."

Progress Check:
You've won when your doubt fears you.

Session 55: Accepting That Nobody Has It Figured Out

Session Goal:
To make peace with universal confusion.

Diagnosis:
Existential Equality Syndrome.

Therapist's Note:
No one knows what they're doing — they just have better fonts.

Recommended Responses:

- "We're all winging it, some with spreadsheets."

- "Life's not a test — it's an open book and I still don't get it."

- "Confusion builds character."

- "I'm lost, but confidently."

Progress Check:
When you can laugh at life's absurdity — that's your diploma.

Session 56: The Fine Art of Saying Nothing — Loudly

Session Goal:
To weaponize silence with elegance.

Diagnosis:
Verbal Economy Syndrome.

Therapist's Note:
You don't always need the last word. The look will do.

Recommended Responses:

- *[Blank stare. Deep sigh. Raised eyebrows.]*

- "Interesting."

- "Noted."

- "I'll let that echo in the silence it deserves."

Progress Check:
You've mastered this when silence makes others explain themselves twice.

Session 57: Choosing Calm Over Clapping Back

Session Goal:
To replace reaction with quiet superiority.

Diagnosis:
Reactive Sarcasm Deprivation.

Therapist's Note:
Calmness is not weakness. It's emotional caffeine.

Recommended Responses:

- "I could respond, but I respect my peace."

- "I'm not ignoring you. I'm prioritizing sanity."

- "You win the argument. I win serenity."

- "Maturity feels weird, but I'm getting used to it."

Progress Check:
You're cured when your silence ruins their mood more than your words ever could.

Session 58: Scripted Grace — How to Exit Dumb Conversations Beautifully

---

Session Goal:
To leave nonsense behind without looking smug.

Diagnosis:
Pointless Dialogue Fatigue.

Therapist's Note:
You can't save everyone. Especially mid-sentence.

Recommended Responses:

- "This has been... enlightening."

- "I suddenly remembered that my plants need emotional support."

- "You've given me a lot to ignore — thank you."

- "I'll circle back .. never."

Progress Check:
If your exit leaves peace and confusion behind, you've graduated.

Session 59: Graceful Pettiness — A Masterclass

Session Goal:
To channel irritation into quiet sophistication.

Diagnosis:
Refined Resentment.

Therapist's Note:
Petty can be polished if it's poetic.

Recommended Responses:

- "I adore how confidently you misunderstand things."

- "What an interesting approach to logic."

- "You've outdone yourself — which wasn't hard."

- "Such effort, such results... unrelated."

Progress Check:
You're elite when your pettiness gets applause instead of HR reports.

Session 60: The Science of Looking Busy

Session Goal:
To avoid interruptions without lying.

Diagnosis:
Productivity Theater Syndrome.

Therapist's Note:
Appearing busy is 80% posture, 20% clicking things.

Recommended Responses:

- "I'd love to chat, but I'm in deep thought."

- "Sorry, I'm on a mental deadline."

- "I'm processing data — in my head."

- "I can't. I'm busy pretending to be productive."

Progress Check:
You've made it when no one dares assign you extra work.

Session 61: Polite Emails That Secretly Drip with Fury

Session Goal:
To communicate rage with grammatical precision.

Diagnosis:
Passive-Aggressive Etiquette Disorder.

Therapist's Note:
"Per my last email" is both a phrase and a weapon.

Recommended Responses:

- "Just circling back :)" *(smile = concealed threat)*

- "As previously mentioned…" *(translation: read, you fool)*

- "Happy to clarify (again)."

- "Please advise." *(final boss of frustration)*

Progress Check:
You're fluent when your tone terrifies politely.

Session 62: Energy Conservation for the Emotionally Drained

Session Goal:
To care only when strictly necessary.

Diagnosis:
Compassion Burnout.

Therapist's Note:
You don't owe enthusiasm to everything.

Recommended Responses:

- "That sounds… like a lot."

- "Wow. You're really going through it." *(monotone)*

- "My empathy's buffering."

- "I wish I had the energy to care properly."

Progress Check:
If you can preserve peace without guilt, you're functioning in advanced settings.

Session 63: The Art of Mentally Clocking Out

Session Goal:
To remain physically present but spiritually gone.

Diagnosis:
Cognitive Absenteeism.

Therapist's Note:
Sometimes your brain deserves paid time off.

Recommended Responses:

- "Fascinating." *(while thinking about lunch)*

- "Hmm." *(universal filler word for survival)*

- "Please, go on." *(no memory will be retained)*

- "I'm here, just not emotionally."

Progress Check:
You've achieved mastery when no one notices your soul has left the room.

Session 64: Cooling Off Before You Set Fire to Something

Session Goal:
To pause before unleashing your inner flamethrower.

Diagnosis:
Impulse Eruption Syndrome.

Therapist's Note:
Anger is valid. Timing is everything.

Recommended Responses:

- "Give me a moment — I'm rebooting civility."

- "Let's revisit this when my tone isn't a weapon."

- "Breathing in... still murderous, but calmer."

- "I'll respond after my blood pressure subsides."

Progress Check:
You've evolved when you delay chaos without denying it.

Session 65: Saying Goodbye to the Need for Revenge

Session Goal:
To let go — but dramatically.

Diagnosis:
Closure Deficiency.

Therapist's Note:
Forgiveness is optional; indifference is luxury.

Recommended Responses:

- "I've outgrown the urge to care."

- "Revenge takes effort. I prefer peace — and better lighting."

- "My silence is your consequence."

- "Some bridges burn themselves. I just enjoy the view."

Progress Check:
When you can move on without a victory speech, you're free.

Final Progress Check:

If you've made it this far without arguing with your book, congratulations — you're officially fluent in **diplomatic sarcasm**.

Your next step?
Graduation from therapy. With homework.

Therapist's Note:
If this book improved your emotional stability by at least 2%, you owe it to humanity to share your progress.

Scan below to leave your "therapy feedback" (Amazon review).
Tell the world which Session cured your sarcasm deprivation, or which one you still need a refill of.

Diplomatic Tip: Reviews are free — unlike real therapy.

Next Session: Advanced Emotional Management

Because sometimes, words aren't enough — you need to color your frustration.

Continue your treatment with
Sarcasm Therapy for the Burned Out Soul: A Monochrome Coloring Book with Sassy Sayings for Stress Relief and Corporate Survival
A stress relief program featuring mind-melting patterns, snarky affirmations,
and zero need for small talk.

Scan this to see it on Amazon.

Diplomatic Tip: It's cheaper than therapy and more satisfying than explaining yourself.

Session Complete.
Now breathe. Smile. And be quietly superior.

- Casper Frankie Shard

Printed in Dunstable, United Kingdom